# The 5-Minute Author

## HOW TO WRITE A NOVEL

SONJA DEWING

PLOT DUCKIES PUBLISHING

ISBN 978-1-7335964-1-1

Updated 2024

# Acknowledgments

This journey I've taken – I couldn't have gotten this far without the help of some awesome people and organizations – ABQID, Creative Startups, and FatPipe ABQ sent me the right direction. My friend and fellow author, Elisabeth Loya, kept me grounded, which is really hard to do. And, Bruce Pitt has been a great mentor and kept me on task.

# Quick Intro

Welcome to *The 5 Minute Author: how to Write a Novel (third edition!).* I'm Sonja Dewing, and I'm looking forward to accompanying you on this writing journey.

Here's a quick note on how to use this book. The idea is for you to read a short chapter and each chapter should take about five minutes or less a day. I'll cover everything from finding an idea for your story to even how to write a sex scene. Each chapter includes ideas, insights, and inspiration from me, and then you find ten to twenty-five minutes a day to write.

I know that even ten minutes a day can end up being a big commitment, but because you purchased this book, I'm willing to bet that you have the drive to find those ten minutes or more. You're here to write, and I'm here to guide you.

And how am I qualified to help? I know what it takes to write a novel. I've written five and published three, with more on the way. I also run "Write a Book" events in February and November. That means that every November, I help people who feel stuck get through writing their novels.

And I know you can do it because I've seen a lot of other people make it happen. So, let's get started, you writer, you.

Now, if you're still not sure you can do this writing thing, I will share a story. I was backpacking with my best friend, Rebecca, in the Pecos Wilderness near Santa Fe. We had been out for three days after camping near an alpine lake. I was exhausted. My backpack was heavy--at least it felt that way after carrying it for three days. Both of us were toting our tents, clothes to stay warm in the quick changing temperatures of the mountains, water, food, and everything else needed for a long backpacking trip. I wasn't even sure I could make it all the way to the parking lot and all I could think about was getting home and ordering pizza and a big glass of ice cold soda. We were on our way back, about three miles from the parking lot, when Rebecca turned to say something, and she tripped on a tree root in the trail. She collapsed like a deck of cards.

I ran to her and immediately saw that her right foot was twisted the wrong way. Her right ankle was broken and her left was sprained. I hated seeing her in such pain.

Now, one thing you might not know is that there is no cell phone service in the Pecos Wilderness. Suddenly, I had a mission. I made her as comfortable as I could, then sprinted three miles of mountain trail to the parking lot, jumped in the car, drove until I found cell reception, contacted emergency services, met their crew at the parking lot, then led the EMTs up to her location.

Three hours later, the team of volunteer firemen carried her three miles to the parking lot. Her mother was waiting. She hugged Rebecca and watched as they loaded her into the ambulance, then she handed me a cold hot dog from Sonic, which I really appreciated.

And just so you know, Rebecca turned out fine. Since she recovered from the broken ankle we've been on more backpacking trips and even snowshoeing.

Life has unexpected surprises in store for all us--but also teaches us. That was seven hours that I kept going beyond what I thought I could have done. We really have so much more energy, power, and stamina than we think we do, especially when we have a mission or a goal in mind.

Which is why I realized that I had more to give and more that I could accomplish. Because when everyone else believes they've done enough, that's when I'm doing more. And guess what? You can too. I know you can. You can find those ten minutes or maybe a little more.

Before we get started, I want you to do a little exercise. You'll need a pen and a sticky note or a piece of paper.

I want you to write these four words: "I am a writer."

Because the moment you start your story, that's who you are, and I want you to remember that as you progress. Put that note somewhere you'll see it every day.

# Ideas for Your Story

Do you already have an idea for your novel? That's awesome! If that's the case, you can move on to chapter three.

But what if you don't have a solid idea yet? If that's the case, let's do a little universe searching for that story idea before we dive into writing.

What I want to suggest first is that you chase your curiosity. What I mean is, is there something that you have an interest in?

For example, the idea for my novel, *Toy of the Gods*, started when I was watching a documentary about the Amazon and how the river is too shallow in places for a boat to travel. That even travelers in canoes have to get out to cross sandbars. That started me thinking: What if there was a boat that could travel the Amazon River? What would it look like, how would it work, and who would take that journey?

Those simple questions started me on a 73,000 word novel about adventurous tourists finding themselves stranded in the Amazon by an Inca god. At the time I started, I had no idea where that story would take me, and I definitely didn't think there would be a god in there. Now, that story has led me to a sequel.

Is there something right now that you've been wondering about? Something that stirs a story? Some TV show, movie, book, story on the news, that peaked your interest on a certain subject? If so, write it down, and do some research.

What else might help you find a story idea?

Look at art. I was looking at hand-printed art the other day. Images of insects in beautiful detail with complex backgrounds. It stirred an idea, but I have enough stories to write right now, so I decided not to chase that idea. Maybe something will stir in you when you look at art. Go check out a local gallery, art show, or museum.

Once you walk through a gallery or other art location, if you still don't have any ideas stirring, walk away from the problem for a bit. In other words, forget that you're looking for a story idea, and go do something else. That something else should be something relaxing and simple, like coloring in a coloring book or knitting or even taking a shower. Definitely don't turn on the TV or get onto social media. Those things feed your brain in a way that limits your creative thoughts. So, just for a while, give media a break, and do something off-line.

Another option is to give yourself prompts for your story. For example, the company NYC Midnight has a flash fiction challenge every year where they assign everyone specific prompts to use for a story. They assign you a genre, a location, and an item to use in the story. In this case, consider assigning yourself a series of prompts.

Play a game of Scrabble or Words with Friends, and consider using the words on the board at the end of the game as required words in a story. That might spur an idea for a novel. Another strategy is a role-playing game. Try getting involved, and see if it inspires a new story.

Here's another idea: What about fan fiction? Is there a story you loved that you want to continue? Or perhaps a side character from a novel or story, and you'd like to see their adventures? Try running with that as your story.

So, that's your assignment for today. Find your curiosity and chase an idea. There's an amazing world of ideas out there.

# Get Organized

I hope you're excited to start on your next writing journey. While you're working on your story, I'm working on my next one too so, I know the future will be wonderful and terrible! It will be unexpected and sometimes tedious. At times, you'll feel that you've written something brilliant, and at other times, it's the worst drivel you've ever thought possible.

You're probably wondering: If the journey is that much of a roller coaster, why write? Well, If you've gotten this far, you probably have a story inside you waiting to burst out or you have the interest to write - and you should follow that interest! Besides, in the end, you'll have written that story. You'll have created something.

## Writing Anywhere

While you're writing for those ten to twenty-five

minutes a day don't feel that you have to use a laptop. You can do your writing using a voice to text-app on your phone or a recording app. You can type it into your phone's notes while you're riding the train (which, if you have an iPhone and a Mac, you could simply copy and paste from the notes program into a Word or Scrivener program). Or you could hand-write it into a notebook.

But at some point, you'll need to put it into an electronic document, especially if you plan to edit, share, or publish your novel.

## Get Organized

Now, let's talk about getting organized. I suggest you put the following items together:

- Notebook and pen. The reason for these will come apparent after listening to the chapter on creative ideas. But keep in mind, we remember things better when we write them down, and why not be kind to our brain and the creative process by making remembering easier.
- Laptop with a program so that you can eventually put the story down electronically. I highly suggest Scrivener (https://www. literatureandlatte.com/scrivener-affiliate. html?fpr=sonja75): It keeps all of your information about your story organized,

including research and character information. It also has some fun things like a name generator and a program that tells you what words you used the most in each chapter, which comes in handy when you start editing.

- A support system in place. At a minimum, I suggest you find at least one person who will support you in this journey, who will applaud you when you've made progress on your story.

- A timer. I talk about that in the chapter "Sprint like you mean it." Basically, a silent timer is perfect. For example, if you are timing yourself for say, ten minutes, and suddenly you're on a roll, you don't want have to stop to turn off a timer. It's just there to glance at it if you need it. So I'm talking about one of those quaint sand timers.

- A reward for the future. What will you give yourself when you've written for thirty days straight? Put something on your list. Maybe it's a book you want to read, a visit to a chocolate shop, or renting a movie. Give yourself something special to look forward to.

Now, for the next ten to twenty-five minutes, I suggest you get organized before moving to the next chapter. In the next chapter, we'll work through how to organize your story for the work ahead.

So remember, you'll need: notebook and pen, laptop, a support system, a timer, and a reward. I look forward to connecting again tomorrow. Time to get organized!

# The Story Prep

I think it's a good idea to have an outline for your novel. But when I say outline, I'm not talking about some rigid structure like the outlines you may have created in high school. The structure or outline you build for your story is what will work for you the best. So, instead of saying outline, let's call it a road map.

You're embarking on an epic journey, so why not make yourself a road map? Besides, if you already have some things figured out before you actually start writing, the less you'll have to stop and plan.

Don't worry if you don't know everything that will happen in the story, but you can jot down as much as you can think of, and more will come later as you're writing.

How to create your road map? There are several options. You could:

- Create a beginning-to-end linear map.

- Create a mind map that connects relevant ideas and scenes.
- Write a paragraph that creates the theme and ideas behind the story.

What do I do? I use a couple of different methods before I get started. To begin, I tend to have one or two vital scenes to start with and work from there, so I actually prefer to start out with a mind map. I use Coggle.it. It's an online mind-mapping tool with a free option that's still pretty powerful.

For example, for the third book in my "Idol Maker" series, *Castoffs of the Gods*, it all started with a flash of a scene. John Holbrook is back in the Amazon, searching for the final resting place of his ancestor, Benedict Cecil Spafford. He comes across the creatures left behind by an Inca god. Everything else that happens in the story needs to build on and from that idea.

Once I've mapped out a bunch of ideas in a mind map, I'll create a series of scene titles in Scrivener. If you don't have Scrivener, you might create different pages in a Word document. Title each page with the scene you have in mind and make any notes on the page with your initial ideas.

Another option for your road map is to use a program like Excel to create a list of scenes.

And here's something that tends to blow people's

minds when I say it. Don't worry if you don't know the opening scene of the novel. Work with what you know, and **start your story wherever you want**. You don't have to begin at the beginning; that will usually come later. But if you do know the beginning, feel free to start with that scene.

And why do I call these "scenes" instead of "chapters"? Because to me, a scene might be able to stand on its own, or it might need to be paired with another scene to create a whole chapter. For example, the second chapter in my first novel is broken up into four scenes in Scrivener. The scenes are: Leslie wakes up in the eco-resort, she explores the grounds, she enjoys breakfast, she chases a burglar. Each of those are a scene, but they don't stand on their own as a chapter. However, by breaking them into scenes, I can move them around when I get to editing.

Now, back to that road map.

It's likely that you've had bursts of ideas of what is going to happen in the story. Write down those scenes in a way that makes sense to you--whether that's a mind map, an Excel spreadsheet, or handwritten in a notebook-- and don't worry if they are not in any particular order.

With me, I know that John Holbrook is in the Amazon, heading toward his destination. He thinks he knows exactly what to expect on his journey. The truth is, he has yet to see the worst that the Amazon can throw at him--and we see that forces are moving against him.

I enter that information in the center of my mind map and build everything from there. One idea that came next is that I know that my main characters, Leslie Kicklighter and AJ Bluehorse, eventually will join forces to search for him.

In this case, I think I know how this story will start. In the thick of the Amazon with John. However, I don't know how it will end. That's part of the fun of writing a project. More than likely, it'll take on a life of its own.

Now it's your turn. Take the ideas you came up with for your novel in the last section, and think of the kinds of scenes that might make them come to life. Tomorrow we'll dive into preparing your characters.

# The Basics of Your Characters

Hello, and welcome back!

Today, I want to talk about mapping out the background for your characters. This is a way to organize your ideas about each character in your story.

The reason for this is that it breathes more life into your characters. Knowing the basics of their backgrounds will help you as you build the story. For example, if you have a better handle on their background, you'll have a better idea for how your characters will react in certain situations, because a character who grew up in Brooklyn and learned how to box versus a character who grew up in France and learned ballet more than likely will react differently when confronted with an aggressive giant vampire bat.

This is also helpful if you have several characters to keep track of, and it helps you to find ways to make each character stand out.

I will mention Scrivener again because I really like its character section. If you happen to have Scrivener and you create a new character under the character folder in your file, they have nine questions ready for you to respond to about your character, which is a helpful start. What's nice about having these files in Scrivener is that you can keep track of each of your characters, and if you have a character who only shows up once in a while in the story, you can just scroll to the folders in your file and find out how the name is spelled. I use that method for my minor characters.

The list of questions about your character that I'm going to share with you is not all encompassing. So if you're writing a western, maybe you want to add to the list the character's favorite weapons. All of which can help you with continuity. You certainly don't want to mention a six-shooter in one scene and then suddenly your character is carrying a musket in the next scene.

You could also develop a character profile for the weapons themselves. That all depends on how important they are to the story. For example, if your story centered around a sword like Excalibur, you might want to write a character outline that develops the background of the sword. It might become important throughout the story, especially if Excalibur has an attitude, which it probably would. With a character profile, you could come up with what kind of attitude it has. Where has it been throughout its history? Was it alone in a cave for many years and gone a little insane? Does it have a thing for scabbards? One would think it might.

And, when the time comes to edit, it helps to have a finalized list of your characters' traits. When you first start your story, your character might have a mustache, but you decide later that it doesn't work, so then you'll change it and update your character outline. When you're ready to edit, you can go back to your updated character traits and fix all the scenes with the mustache. No more mustache twirling for this character!

And don't worry if you aren't spending time writing the actual story yet. Even if you're spending time writing your character descriptions, it's still writing, and you're making progress on your story, so don't feel that you're off track. In fact, you're not. Knowing your characters better means you'll write more believable scenes with those characters.

Here's a list of things to consider for your character:

- Name,
- occupation,
- marital status,
- gender identification,
- clothes they normally wear,
- health status,
- appearance,
- identifiers such as mannerisms they have or props they are often seen with,
- education or vocation,

- employment history,
- past relationships,
- current relationships,
- ethnicity,
- home,
- hobbies,
- religious beliefs,
- political beliefs,
- ambitions/desires/and long-term goals,
- fears and superstitions,
- favorite places,
- temperament,
- how they speak,
- character flaws (I'll go over more about that later but see if you can come up with something today.)

Your goal today is of course to write up the backgrounds to your characters, and add to the list of questions anything else that's important.

If you'd like a workbook to help you get into more details and help you develop characters in 30 minutes or less, you can find it at my business website: https://womensthrillerwriters.com/character-development/

Good luck, and good character writing!

# Sprint Like You Mean It

~~~

Congratulations! You're onto the next day of creating, and we'll get into writing. Today, I'm sharing a way that I tend to write and that works for me. I'm hoping it helps you too.

I mentioned before that I run a "Write a Book" event in February and November. During the event, I help people write novels in 30 days. The good news is I'm not asking you to write a full novel in a month. I'm just asking you to find the time where you can for writing and keep making progress on your story one day at a time.

The key to reaching your goal is to use writing sprints. Not only that, when you sprint as fast as you can, your story starts to surprise you. I've had sprints where I started a scene or chapter, and I had no idea what was going to happen, and suddenly it took a fun and creative turn.

This is what I want you to do. I want you to set a timer for 10 minutes. As soon as that timer starts, start writing as fast as you can--whether it's dictating into your phone, typing into your phone, typing on your laptop, or handwriting in a notebook.

Where do you start? Start anywhere. That's right. You don't have to start at the beginning of the novel. In fact, many writers skip around as ideas come to them. Plus, this book is meant for you to skip around to different parts of your story. You can always clean up the ideas when you edit much, much later.

When that ten minutes is over, if you feel you have more to say, keep writing. Your goal today is to write anywhere from ten to twenty-five minutes. You've got this.

Hopefully, you take this sprinting practice and use it. Don't feel you have to sprint all the time; in fact, I suggest sprinting once a week. Keep in mind, the faster we get everything down in writing, the sooner we finish.

Good luck, and I hope you find some unexpected twists and turns when you sprint your story.

# Don't Edit

Maxwell Perkins was an American book editor who discovered authors Thomas Wolfe and Ernest Hemingway. He once said, "Just get it down on paper, and then we'll see what to do with it."

In my opinion, that's a perfect idea. When you're writing your first draft, don't worry about editing. Don't hit the backspace, and don't read what you just wrote. Keep moving the story forward.

Why? First of all, once you have that story flow going, you don't want to stop that flow by editing. The initial idea and story are the most important things to get down, now.

Second, as a goal, finishing your first draft is much closer if you're focused on getting through it the first time.

Think about it. If you start editing now, when you aren't finished yet, it will take longer to get to the end of the story. In fact, it will feel like it's taking forever to get to the end. And let me tell you that that information comes from my own experience. I used to edit as I wrote, and I would begin to lose interest in a story. However, if I get all the way through to the end for my first draft, I feel much more accomplished, and then I'm ready for the editing of an ugly, ugly story. OK, maybe it's not double ugly, but our first draft is allowed to be ugly.

Third, it helps to separate yourself from the story you've written before you start the editing process. This way, you'll create some objectivity before you take another look at it. Creating a different set of time to write and then later edit is a good way to kind of forget what you first created and come back with fresh eyes. This includes fixing story structure and plot.

Just get the naked story on paper. Worry about dressing it up later. Enough analogies, right?

**Save the Research for Later**

Here's a tip about writing when you don't know the name of something or you realize you need more research, put in a filler instead of stopping. For example, in my novel, *Gamble of the Gods* I knew I was going to add a new Navajo character, but I didn't have time to come up with a name yet, so instead of stopping to research and pick a name, I simply put in filler so I'd know to go back and edit and then add that information later. The filler I like to use is a special character (and when I talk about a special character, I'm not talking about a person but a button on my keyboard).

In my case, I use a hashtag, also known as the pound

sign, in places where I know I need to add or change something. The hashtag is something I don't usually use in my writing so it sticks out when I'm editing or I can spot it quickly when I go back.

Another thing I do, because I'm using Scrivener, each scene gets its own new section. That way, if I do go back to read anything, it's so I can remember where I was when I last left off. I don't back up to any other sections and read anything so I can make sure I don't try to edit anything.

My friend and fellow author, Elisabeth Loya, says, "I close my eyes during sprints. But if you need to look at the keyboard, you can cover your monitor with a sheet of paper or a notebook. (Two sheets taped together on the long side works well for a laptop). If you need to go back and read a section, just uncover, read, replace cursor, replace cover, and keep going."

Writer Anne Goralczyk says she uses music challenges. "I listen to epic music. I write until the music is over. No going back to fix typos or editing."

And writer Thomas Adkins says, "Having place markers for me helps quell my inner editor by acknowledging my mistakes and making little road markers to make coming back to clean everything up easier."

If you can, talk with your inner editor, and let that inner editor know that they will have their time, just not today. So good luck, and get writing!

# What Happens when You Write Everyday

T.S. Eliot said, "Writing every day is a way of keeping the engine running, and then something good may come out of it."

There are indeed good things that come out of writing every day. When you work on a creative project daily, your creative mind begins to see new connections, threads, plots, and thus weaves a more intricate story.

Before we talk more about what happens when you find a writing habit, let me tell you what can happen if you don't write.

I'm about to share a personal story, a true story, and a true failing of my own. I've always been a writer. As far back as I can remember, I used to sit in my window, dream of other worlds, and write about them. I kept it up until I was in my twenties, and then I met a man who I thought was my Prince Charming. He was charismatic, and within a month of dating, he talked me into moving in with him.

You know how truth is stranger than fiction? It's certainly strange for me to look back now. He would get upset if I was at my computer writing while he was watching TV. So, little by little, I stopped sitting at my computer writing and started sitting next to him at the TV, holding his hand. Bit by bit, I could feel my creative ideas slipping away. Whole stories would show up in my head, but I would shake them away because I had no time for them.

There were many signs that he was far from my Prince Charming, but it took me a whole year before I began to realize that and how unhappy I was.

Once I was out of that relationship, it took me years to get back to writing again. I was honestly afraid that I'd never be creative again and that I'd never be able to write a truly good story.

I was so wrong. I've written some of my favorite pieces since I resumed writing but it took time and practice to get back into the habit. I've received five-star reviews from complete strangers, and several awards for my creative writing. That meant a lot to me in my journey for creativity.

So, I don't want you to hold the hand of that thing that's stopping you from writing. I don't want you to plunge into the despair I was in. Walk away from that, and keep up writing.

What happens if you write every day? From experience, I know you might think you know everything important that will happen in your story, but then suddenly you come up with a totally new thread or exciting moment you never saw coming. And it all works out so much better when you've worked on the story day by day, even if it is just ten minutes.

So there you go. Don't give up on yourself, because I'm not giving up on you. And don't worry about me and my sad story, because we all have our sad stories, and I'm much happier now.

Now, it's your turn to go out there and write.

# Character Flaws

Hello! I'm glad you're back, and I hope you're making progress on your story. If not, don't worry, keep writing, and you'll make progress. We're only a few days in, and we have plenty of awesome writing days ahead of us.

Today, I want to share information about the flaws driving your main character. If you filled out the character outline, you probably have a good handle on your character's background, but what does your character struggle with?

Specifically, a character flaw refers to the things that are not perfect about your character, especially your main character. The idea is that you can throw situations at your character that challenge their flaw, and maybe they learn from those situations.

For example, I'll share a real flawed person I met on my travels in South America. My best friend and I had just made it to the island of Isla Bastimentos in Panama, and we met Biff, who was staying at our hostel.

We played a few card games together, and in that short span, there were so many flaws I could point out:

- He carried a tape player with him and was playing songs loudly that had hateful lyrics.
- Biff was drinking a nonalcoholic beer but pretending to be drunk. I think this was in some way to get other people to underestimate him.
- He treated his friend poorly. Kevin was a South American kid who was hanging out with Biff, but Biff used gay slurs and stereotyped ideas to address Kevin, such as calling him Fernando.
- He mentioned how he had a fantastic boat and that we should all go check it out with him. (I add that in because I don't think he had a boat, and it was creepy the way he suggested we should go with him to the dock.)

FYI: We did not go anywhere with Biff, and you definitely don't want your main character riddled with a bunch of character flaws. What you do want is to choose one flaw to carry through the book.

If I was going to take one of these flaws and apply it to a main character, it would probably be the drinking. Maybe I have a hardened private Investigator who doesn't want anyone to know she doesn't drink and she likes the idea of people underestimating her. She's often seen with a drink in her hand. How can that be a flaw? She would use the "drinking" as a crutch and thinks she needs to pretend to be drunk to do her job.

What about your own main character? What might their flaw be? Think about people you know. What are their flaws? How do they act out those flaws? Would any of those work for your character?

Also, keep in mind that some acceptable character traits can turn into flaws. Scrooge McDuck saw himself as frugal and disciplined, but others saw him as miserly and cold-hearted.

Other ideas for character flaws? Here are a few:

- A bad habit: Personally, I always think of my own bad habit, which is lots and lots of coffee drinking. I also remember someone telling me about a co-worker who would clip his toenails at the office; his clippings would go flying around the room. Maybe he's secretly a werewolf and had to trim his nails every few hours. At least we hope so.
- Vanity: Like a character who would rather wear a fancy jacket and look beautiful rather than wear a thick, warm jacket and be comfortable, but also conceited and self-serving in their own way.

- Temperamental: Being moody. That someone who everyone tiptoes around to not set off their mood-o-meter.
- Theatrical: Someone who is over the top. For example: a boyfriend who buys his girlfriend a giant, gaudy piece of gold jewelry because it makes him look generous, or someone who has to be the loudest person in the room.

If you're still struggling with an idea for a character flaw, Google it and see how many ideas pop up. Or, people-watch, and see if you can pinpoint someone's flaws, and use that in your story.

If you don't already have a focus for today's writing time, consider coming up with your character's flaw and writing about it. For example, if their flaw is to be rash, write a scene where they are making a rash decision or where they learn that a rash decision isn't always the best choice.

# Reduce Interruptions

Sometimes it can be hard to find time to write, and when we do find it, the rest of the world is competing with our time to create. Plus, research shows that when we end up multitasking, we reduce our productivity. Since you're here to get your writing done, I have some suggestions on ways to reduce the interruptions so you can keep writing:

- Schedule the time. I work out of a co-working space, and everyone knows me. So, when they feel the need to talk, they'll walk on over. Which is fine, except when I'm deep into writing a new chapter and the story ideas are flowing. When I'm going to write, I'll schedule the conference room for thirty minutes so I know I have uninterrupted time alone. If you don't have a conference room, consider moving into a space that reduces access to you from your co-workers or your family. If it's a nice day out, consider heading to the botanical gardens and secreting away at a bench; maybe you have a nearby museum, coffee shop, or even a chair or table in a discreet corner. If none of those options is available, consider talking to the people working around you about the project you're working on, and put up a polite sign that says, "I'm creating, please come back in thirty minutes."

- Time your writing time. Sometimes we create our own interruptions by deciding we're going to do something else real quick, and then we'll get back to writing. Then we end up splitting our time away from the writing. My solution is to set a timer, at a minimum of ten minutes. That ten minutes is your focused writing time. To be honest, once I get going, I usually find that I'll go longer than the ten-minute timer.

- Turn off notifications. Nothing interrupts the flow of work more than if your phone dings at you because someone just commented on your Facebook post. Suddenly, we want to go see what they said, then we end up on Facebook, scrolling through posts, and our writing is pushed aside. To reduce my own time on social media, I turn off all of my notifications. I know that I can go onto social media once in the morning, again at noon, and then in the evening. This saves me so much time. If you aren't sure how much time you spend on social media, you might want to keep a log. I know that when I did that and then restructured my use of social media, I saved about two hours a day. Besides, my life is much simpler without hearing the dings of social notifications.

Reduce online interruptions. Sometimes we need to go online during our precious creative time in order o research something. Or in my case, I love to ask questions to my friends on Facebook and see if they can come up with good ideas. So how do you go online without getting too distracted? Here are some options:

- Chrome extension for Facebook. It used to be that when I would go onto Facebook for a specific reason, I would get entangled in the Facebook feed. I would suddenly find myself watching a cute cat video of this tabby getting into a cat-sized hammock. I call that chasing the squirrel, and things like that would suck up my time. To be honest, I would rather know I spent precious time on my writing than watching that cute cat video. Now, I use The News Feed Eradicator; it's a chrome extension that instead of seeing the newsfeed, you see a wonderfully motivating quote. You can even add your own custom quotes. Just google, "News feed eradicator."

- Limit open tabs. Once upon a time, I would have about eleven tabs open on my Google Chrome. So, when I would go to do research, suddenly I was distracted by all those tabs. So, if you are in the same boat, I suggest you use TabX. It's another Chrome extension that you set to limit the number of tabs you have open. I keep mine at five.
- Close your email. And if there is one tab that distracts the most, it's my email. Do I really need my email open for that short writing time? Nope.

Good luck on reducing interruptions.

There's no assignment today. Get your timer out, and get writing.

# Just Write

Let me share a quote with you. E.L. Doctorow, historical fiction writer, once said, "Writing a novel is like driving a car at night. You can see only as far as your headlights, but you can make the whole trip that way."

It's true. Bit by bit, we move ourselves forward, and eventually we'll make it to the end!

You've been writing for the past nine days. Today, I just want you to write. You probably have plenty of ideas.

Turn on your timer, and get going.

# Internal Forces

You should be proud of yourself. You're gathering ideas, and you're writing. That's your goal, and you're making it happen.

So, don't give up; keep getting that story of yours down. Today, I'm going to dive into internal forces within your character.

Why have an internal struggle or struggles for your character? Conflict and internal struggles create tension and raise the stakes for the character, which creates a deeper story.

Now, internal forces are not the same as your character's flaw. A character flaw is generally something external that others can see. An internal conflict is something the character is struggling with, usually on an emotional level, and can obstruct their objectives, but those around them don't generally notice the struggle.

Let's use Harry Potter as an example. His internal

struggle tends to be living life without parents. It's not a flaw, but it's something his character must struggle with. That struggle appears throughout the story and affects his decisions, like when he realizes his father played Quidditch, Harry puts his heart into playing the game and uses it to honor his father's memory. If you go back and look at the story, you'll see that the struggle affects his decisions in small ways.

Now, if you don't already have an idea of what you're working on today, consider writing a scene that challenges your character with an internal conflict. How to do that?

Here are some ideas for that internal and emotional struggle:

- Your character has to act against their morals and/or ethics. First, let me give you a list of some moral dilemmas: being a vegan who must choose between eating a steak or starving, a trustworthy person who must choose between stealing something they need or dying, someone who is serious about keeping promises but must break one for some reason. What would your character be facing to break their own moral code?
- Give your character a crisis of conscience: For example, did someone else do something your character didn't agree with, but they went along with it, and now they feel guilty? Will

your character do something to fix the situation?

- Have your character make a bad decision due to embarrassment: Think of those crime stories where a person doesn't come forward to show someone is innocent because maybe they were hanging out with their mistress when they saw it go down.

- Give your character a crisis of conscience. In my novel, "Toy of the Gods," Leslie is dealing with such a crisis in that she believes she was the reason her friend was killed in an accident. That fear colors her choices throughout the book, including when she has to make the decision about whether she'll help lead her friends out of the jungle.

Do you have situations you've been through that you could apply to your characters' inner conflict? What internal conflicts have you had to deal with? It's definitely easier to apply situations you're familiar with to your characters because that gives you a sense of reality and the knowledge of how someone would respond.

# Adding More Creative Ideas (The Notebook)

Why not have a stockpile of creative ideas to use when you need them? That's the idea behind the notebook. Especially how I use a notebook.

Sure, I know you probably have a stack of notebooks with ideas, and you probably don't remember where to find specific ideas, which is why I came up with a system that has worked fabulously.

It's also how I came up with my idea for my award-winning flash fiction story, "Something." It's a story about an old man with plenty of time on his hands, so he's sitting in a lawn chair, reading a newspaper, and watching a fence. There's a nail on the fence, and every day, something new appears there. He's not sure if it's magic or something else. The judges gave the story high marks because of its originality. I loved it because I took something from my notebook of ideas and used it for a short, quirky story.

The idea came from real life. My uncle once told me about a nail on his fence and how every day he took the dog for a walk, he'd find something new hanging on the fence. Always something you might find in an old hardware store. At the time, he couldn't figure out where the stuff was coming from.

In my notebook, I collect weird stories--as well as others, but we'll get back to that. So, when a contest came up, I glanced through my notebook and thought I'd try my hand at writing something from that specific idea.

Let's talk more about our notebook. Yes, you could use an app on your phone, such as notes, but research shows that we remember things better when we write them down. Not only that, because I'm asking you to organize your notebook to match your genres and the things you might need, you tend to remember the items better. So when you need to add new ideas to your novel or you want to submit a new story to a contest, you can say, "Let me open up my notebook to weird ideas and see what I have."

The ideal notebook situation is to have at least four or five sticky tabs that mark out your genres that you like to write in. The tabs in my notebook are: sci-fi, weird, humorous, scary, adventure, and characters. I also have a tab for my third novel in the Idol Maker Series.

I take my notebook with me everywhere, and it kind of looks like it: It's a little beat up. It also took some time for me to build up the practice of writing ideas down, but now that I'm in the practice, I've got several pages under each tab, so there are plenty of ideas that I can use in new stories or even in the novel I'm writing now.

My suggestion is to get started adding ideas by thinking about your past. Have you experienced anything matching your genre tabs? For example, under the funny tab, I note that I once carried a giant tuba through a long line at Antiques Roadshow. Not exactly funny, but it definitely has possibilities for a humorous story. Life is stranger than fiction, right? I bet you have some experiences you could immediately add to your notebook.

Other things I add under my ideas are things I overhear in conversations. I once heard a young girl say, "There's this place like California or something and you can eat gazelles." Hmm . . . gazelles.

I also jot down impressions from art. I glanced at a painting once and got this impression of a woman with a tiny, pointy nose who was wearing a dress made of the sea.

Am I worried about sharing these ideas with you? Absolutely not. You're welcome to use these ideas too, because what you write and what I write will be completely different.

So for today, there's no particular prompt or idea for your story-writing time, but I do suggest that you start a notebook, and if you do, use the marked tabs so we can all be organized creatives and have some amazing ideas at our fingertips.

# What else can tell us about a character

_〜の〜_

I really hope you liked the chapter on using your notebook to collect creative ideas. I feel it's the perfect balance between being creative and being a little organized, and it's definitely helped me. I used to have a huge stack of notebooks and never went back to them because they were so disorganized. Those days are over.

Today though, we're going to refocus on character. I know that you already worked on the back story, and you have ideas on how your characters should react in certain situations. Now, we're going to work on those other things that build on our characters.

You can say a lot about a character by sharing their story through their actions and thoughts. It's also through those actions and thoughts that we as readers either like them, love them, or hate them. Remember too, that the things we share with our readers are interpreted by their own experiences.

For example, in Octavia E. Butler's *Parable of the Sower*, Lauren is remembering lying back and gazing at the stars. As a reader, I'm not necessarily imagining her experience, but I'm remembering my own experience and what it was like to see a sky full of stars. By knowing our readers have their own experiences, we can let them fill in some of the details with their own imagination and connect with our characters through familiar things.

If we want to capture our readers, we also want to dive into our characters quickly. For example, in *The Tomb*, part of the Repairman Jack series, we learn about twenty different things about Jack in just the first few pages. We watch as he awakens on his couch after a night of watching his favorite monster movies. We quickly learn that besides liking monster movies, he's fastidious about his movie collection, but the rest of his place is a dusty, cluttered mess filled with antiques. Anyone who's ever fallen asleep on the couch watching a movie or loves monster movies will connect with Jack as a character.

Another example: In just the first two pages of *Parable of the Sower*, we learn the main character is under stress, that it's her birthday, she has a stepmother, she has a recurring dream, and that this character is just fifteen years old. What could be causing stress on a young woman's birthday? The story begs us to keep reading and to see what happens.

What is it that drew you to a particular character in a story? I suggest you take a look at one of your favorite novels and find a chapter that dives into a character. Note how many things you see that reveal the character, what things make you feel for or connect with that character. How much does the writer reveal about a character within a few pages?

Other things to consider when writing a character's story, things that people use every day can give clues about who they are from their ring tones to their choice of pet to the kind of coffee they order.

How else are characters revealed? Listen in on conversations, and people-watch. What can you discern from what they wear, how they talk, how they interact with the world around them.

For today, write an introduction to your character. This could be a back story that might not appear in your novel, or it might be an early chapter, when you introduce the character to the reader for the first time. What will make us connect with the character?

# Before You Go to Bed

Welcome back! This should be about day fifteen for you if you're doing these one at a time. Congratulations.

There are ideas about breaking through blocks throughout this audiobook. One that we're going to cover today is to use sleep as your problem solver.

We often do find that while we're sleeping, we'll come up with a solution for a problem. And it's not just a feeling we have.

There's proof in a research study published in the Journal of Sleep Research that was conducted by the University of Alberta and the University of Montreal.

For a week, four hundred and seventy Canadian students noted down specific events that they could recall throughout the week; they also noted down their dreams. Especially those dreams on the night following remembered events. Researchers found that their dreams tended to reflect problem resolution and positive emotions. This suggested that the dreams helped people work through their difficulties.

Researchers called in independent individuals to review the data from the students. What they found was that dreams do indeed offer solutions to our dilemmas. Not only that, our dreams offered solutions to problems anywhere from the next day up to seven days later.

Here's a direct quote from one of the researchers. "This suggests an ongoing effort to resolve a problem in dreams during the week following the emergence of that problem. The dreams themselves are a kind of treatment," Dr. Don Kuiken said.

What does it all mean? It means that we can use our dreams to help us solve our writing blocks.

How does it work? Before you go to bed, think about the block you're having. Are you stuck on what a character should do next? What scene or plot should be coming up? Think about that, even write it down in a notebook or a piece of paper before you fall asleep. Because when we write something in pen and paper, we are more likely to remember it.

Then, make sure to have that notebook and pen nearby when you wake up in the morning so you can jot down any ideas that might come to you.

To be honest, I've also gotten whole new story ideas from my dreams, so I generally keep a notebook next to my bed so I can record those ideas before I forget them.

But right now, you probably aren't ready to go to sleep. You're probably read to write. So, get your timer out, and get writing.

# Change Writing Locations

Today, I have a challenge for you. You've probably been writing in the same location. Today, or maybe tomorrow, whatever's convenient, I want you to try a new location. A bench in a park, a seat in the hallway of a convention center, a new coffee shop.

Why? New spaces have a different energy about them. You might notice things and come up with ideas for your story that you wouldn't have found in your normal space. Plus, you might just find your next favorite writing spot.

Some of my favorites? A bench at the zoo, a seat at a co-working space, or the corner of a brewery.

One thing I don't do when I write creatively is I don't sit at my work desk that I rent at a co-working space. I'll write blog posts, nonfiction, web copy, but when it comes to fiction, I prefer to sit in a different seat or be in a different place so I can focus on creativity and not on technical work. I just prefer to have that separated space.

Also, don't forget to schedule your time to write. Put it on your calendar. If you write it down, you're more likely to do it.

I tend to write mostly in the evening, which is when I feel the most creative, but I also like taking time here and there to write in the morning. Your best bet is to find what works for you.

Once you check out your new writing space, your challenge is to incorporate something from the space into your story. It could be a person, the space itself, or even something as small as a coffee mug. Good luck on today's writing, and I hope you find the perfect place to write.

# Duckie Deblocking

Have you heard about Rubber Duck Debugging?

If you're not a programmer, this might come as a new thing to you. The idea comes from a book, *The Pragmatic Programmer*. In the book, a programmer uses a rubber duck to debug code by explaining it to the duck. Have you ever noticed that when you talk something out loud you can sometimes find an answer? That's the idea behind talking to a rubber duckie.

And it's a real thing.

A variety of research studies have shown that talking out loud helps us solve problems faster. For example, research published in the Journal of Research in Educational Psychology found that discussing problems out loud was the fastest way to correctly solve a mathematical problem.

I'm going to appropriate that idea for us writers and

call it Duckie Deblocking so we can solve our writing problems.

If you don't have a Plot Duckie, you can find them online or find yourself some inanimate object, maybe a plush unicorn, that you can have an honest one-on-one with. This way, you're not just talking out loud; you're talking to something that's a great listener.

How does this work? When we talk through our writing problem, we want to focus on what the problem is and come up with as many options as we can that could possibly fix the problem, as well as *how* that would fix the problem.

For example, I had a problem in my storyline for "*Toy of the Gods.*" In the story, an entrepreneur has invented a new way to travel, and he wants to promote it by traveling on the Amazon River.

The problem was the entrepreneur, John Holbrook, had all kinds of reasons to halt his project. I knew that he needed a deeper reason to make his trip happen than just a business need. He would be a fool to put all his eggs in one basket, leaving all his hopes in his one ship, *Toy of the Gods*.

So, on a long car ride, I had a serious talk with my Plot Duckie, Bob. By talking each of the problems out loud with Bob and the possible fixes, I came up with ideas that worked well with the storyline and made the story better. That all started the idea of John being a distant relative of a 1920's British explorer and grew from there.

I think you'll be surprised to find what answers you get when you use Duckie Deblocking. Now, go and write for ten to twenty-five minutes, and if you come to a problem, find a quiet space and have a serious conversation with your duckie.

# Dialogue

Ever listen in on conversations at a coffee shop? FYI: If you put on some headphones as if you're listening to music, most people won't care what they say around you. Not that I've done that.

OK, I have. But it's part of learning and getting to know how real conversations go.

Listening to real conversation helps us think about how to write dialogue. I would just suggest to keep out the boring bits.

Dialogue is a great way to move your plot forward as well as to throw in some character development.

What should we consider when we're working our way through a conversation among our characters?

When you first created your character information, one of the things you should have considered was how they speak differently. It doesn't have to be something extreme. For example, I have an older character in my novel who uses words that are not as common anymore. I also have a character who uses "so" or "well" at the beginning of most of his sentences. Think about the character and what would work for them. Are they from the South and have a twang? Or maybe they have a different rhythm in the way they speak.

Another thing to consider: Even though you might listen in on conversations in a coffee shop, readers don't generally enjoy reading about conversations that happen in a coffee shop. Think about the first meeting of Harry, Ron, and Hermione in the movie version of "Harry Potter." It occurred on the train on their way to Hogwarts, with the countryside moving by and leaping chocolate frogs in the hallway. What would that scene have been like if they had just met in a coffee shop in downtown London? Definitely not as entertaining or as interactive.

Or, consider the scene in one of my favorite books, Julie Czerneda's novel "Survival," in which two characters have a conversation while the main character is doing her work (she's a biologist and she's monitoring a stream outdoors). We get to see the main character in her element, and the meet-up conversation takes an interesting turn in the end when she pushes the other character into the water.

In both of those cases, the scenes are also sharing information about the world and characters to the reader. What about your characters? Is there a conversation they could have that would be engaging in a more active scene.

What in the scene could share some details about your world to the reader?

Also consider, what in the plot can you further along with this conversation? What new thing will the reader learn?

And if you've got more than two characters in the scene, don't forget to tell the reader where the other characters are, what they're doing, or maybe they join the conversation.

Need some prompts for the conversation? Here are some ideas:

- Someone noticed something unusual and wanted to tell someone else.
- A character has unexpected news.
- A character has a question for another character.
- Your main character is angry and needs to have it out with another character.

Now, stop a second, and don't worry about all those things I just said about dialogue. What I want you to do is write a scene of dialogue with your characters. Just write it. You can always fix the scene later when you edit.

# Interview Your Character

Have you had the chance to really get to know your main character? Or maybe you're struggling with one of the minor characters?

If you are, here are some things to write about when you need new inspiration about your character.

One option is to write a short story about your character in a timeline before the novel started. Exposing your character to a different time and experience can help you get to know them even better.

Another option is to sit down, and interview your character. Does that sound weird? Well, it might, but it works.

Maybe interview them as if you're a detective, and you've got your character in a hot interview room with light blaring in their eyes. Or maybe you're a journalist with a list of questions for your character. So, come up with some questions for your character.

Start off easy, and then move onto more difficult questions.

Can a character talk back to you? Yes.

For example, Diana Gabaldon once said that every time she tried to write the character of Claire Randall in "Outlander," the character came out too sassy for a 18th-century woman from Scotland. She finally had to write her as a modern woman, and the only way she could make that work was to have her come from the future.

Sometimes, our characters can surprise us.

Want some questions to start off with? Here are a few:

- What's your favorite ice cream?
- Why is that your favorite flavor?
- Did you ever ditch school?
- How do you feel about smoking?
- Have you ever been arrested?
- Who was your first kiss?
- What's your favorite thing about your work?
- If you could hang out somewhere all day, where would it be?
- Did you ever learn a new language?
- Are you a germaphobe?
- Have you ever been in the hospital?

There you go. Now come up with your own list of questions, then "sit" down with your character, and ask away. Incorporate items from the interview into a new chapter for your book.

# Using Food as a Device

Hello again. Today, let's talk about food. What I want to get into is using food as an add-in to scenes and character development.

One great example of food as an integral use in a novel is Dianne Mott Davidson's series about a mystery-solving caterer named Goldy Bear. It all starts with the first novel, *Catering to Nobody*.

In the novels, Goldy's food is enjoyed by everyone; she often samples her own food, and sometimes the reader gets to feel what it's like to mix and bake a recipe. All these descriptions and experiences can add to a story in a variety of ways. In this example, it also let's us see deeper into Goldy's character.

It makes sense that all of her stories feature food and even include real recipes because Goldy is a food focused character. Of course, you don't need to go to that extreme if you're not into recipes or cooking. In Goldy's case, we learn a lot about Goldy through her cooking, her love of cooking, and of course, by watching her solve mysteries while making a go of a catering business.

Explaining meals can sometimes bring out more information about your character. For example, do they have a big family around the table on holidays and have a variety of food? Or is your main character someone who buys a tiny one-person Cornish game hen, and that's their holiday meal? Or maybe they have a turkey TV dinner. Better yet, maybe they run off to a hostel in a remote town and spend their holiday at a potluck with people from around the world. And if you haven't experienced that, I highly recommend it.

How can writing about food develop character? In Goldy's case, it's a chance for us to see her in action-- creating and cooking. We can also learn more about Goldy by the recipes she chooses. Maybe she'll be nostalgic for a dessert she had at a friend's wedding, and while she's trying to figure out a recipe for it she can walk through her memories of the wedding. We can learn more about Goldy by seeing what happened at the wedding, what she enjoyed, what things didn't go right and how she reacted to them. It gives us another chance to look into the history and inside the mind of a character.

You can also develop the flavor and character of a location. If you're writing a story based in Costa Rica, you'd probably want your character to savor a plate of eggs, cheese, and gallo pinto (which is rice and beans). If you're in almost any South American country, you'd want to include something about the variety and accessibility to fresh fruit juice and ripe fruit. If your character is in China, maybe they're enjoying a family meal with rice and vegetables.

Here are some things to think about:

- What food goes with your story and your characters?
- When your character is in a restaurant, what kind of food attracts their attention?
- What aromas make them hungry?
- What food stenches repulse them?
- If they are sitting in a restaurant for breakfast, do they go for a bowl of granola or steak and eggs?
- What tastes do they savor or maybe miss?

Now, set your timer, and I want you to write a food scene. It could be a picnic, restaurant, cooking at home, a barbecue, whatever works for your scene. Include the sights, smells, and tastes of everything going on in the scene.

# Past Expectations

As of today, you'll have been writing for about twenty days. Amazing! I want you to remember that not everyone is willing to have the tenacity to keep going. So, congratulations!

Here's a quick story where I learned to ignore other people's expectations and hopefully encourage you to keep going and don't let anyone tell you what you can or can't do.

Some friends and I were on a seven-day hike on the Appalachian Trail.

On the first few days, I was a little slow, so in the morning my friends would go their faster speed and then wait for me at lunch and then again at dinner. And I was totally fine with that; it meant we could all go at our own pace. The third day started out misty and rainy, a typical Virginia day. The kind of rain you figure will last all day.

We had two choices. We could hike for three miles and

then turn off the trail to find a campsite or we could hike twelve miles to a hostel. We talked about it and agreed we'd go the twelve miles even though it was raining. So we finished our breakfast, packed up, and headed out.

It was the most peaceful and amazing hike of my life. I didn't start worrying until lunchtime because lunch came and went, and I never caught up to my friends. I figured maybe they didn't want to stop in the rain to eat, so they have must have kept going. So I kept going. There were a lot of natural barriers I had to deal with that day. A giant tree (about 6 feet in diameter) had fallen across the trail, and I had to figure out how to get over it on my own. There was a deep creek I had to cross using a skinny tree that had fallen over, and plenty of uphill hiking. But still, no friends in sight. In fact, I came across no one that day until, as the sun was setting and the temperature was dropping, I walked into Bears Den Hostel. I must have looked a mess. I had been hiking all day in the rain, pausing long enough only to nibble on granola.

What had happened to my friends? When they had reached the turnoff at three miles, they started talking and decided they didn't think I could make twelve miles. So they hiked down to the campsite, dropped their gear, then went back to the turnoff to wait for me.

They had underestimated my speed, and by the time they had retraced their steps to the turnoff, I had already passed it.

I am sure that if I had met up with them that day, I would've accepted their expectations of me. As it is, I'm so glad I didn't. When they arrived at the hostel the next day, they told me even then that they couldn't believe I had hiked so far on my own in one day.

So, I'm telling you now. Don't live up to others expectations of you. Make your own.

Honestly, I think you've heard enough from me already. Today, what kind of adventure or in what way can your character blast other people's expectations? Turn on your timer, and get writing.

# Using Setting as a Character

Changing the setting of a scene can drastically change a scene.

Imagine the following:

King Kong, the giant gorilla, is climbing up the tower in New York City. There's mass chaos!

Now imagine the same scene but King Kong is in a small town in Kansas. The gorilla escapes his bonds and runs into the wilds of a Kansas cornfield. He's an easy target for bullets or an airplane. The movie is over pretty quickly.

Or imagine a spaghetti western, but the scene is in a grocery store. That would be a fun story to write, but you can also tell that the feeling evoked in a bright, air-conditioned grocery store isn't the same as a dusty, tumbleweed strewn western landscape.

When I originally wrote *Toy of the Gods*, I had never

been to the Amazon. I wrote the original version of the story based on a little research and a few movies I had seen.

It wasn't until I was ready to edit that my best friend and I spent time in the Amazon at an eco-resort. After visiting there and having a local guide show us the amazing things in the Amazon, I returned to the states and rewrote the book with the Amazon as a character in itself. What's its character? It's like those bombshells from noir films: beautiful yet dangerous in unexpected ways.

Set your scene as best you can to fit your story, but also, don't worry right now about being exactly perfect about your setting. Just write as much as you can now, and worry about fixing details in the editing phase.

Things to consider:

- Can your location be considered an antagonist? Is it prohibiting your character from achieving their objective?
- What quirks exist within your setting? In the Amazon, there are trees that house huge fire ant colonies, razor sharp-toothed yellow piranha in the rivers, and bugs that will bury their larvae in your skin. I'd say those are some quirks.
- Can you compare your setting to a personality? Is it fun and flirty? Dark and stormy? Remote and unsocial? How can you reflect that in your writing?

- What are the sights, smells, and sounds of your setting?
- What is the weather like in your setting? Is the air heavy with humidity? Does the weather change at a moment's notice?
- If your location is imaginary, what does it look like? Is it a secret cave that only your character can find, with dripping water, and glowing rocks? Or is it a purple-hued planet with three moons that smells like cotton candy?
- How does your main character feel about the setting? How do they interact with it?

Now it's time to write. Write a scene that dives into the character of your setting.

# Walk away from Writing

Irving Stone, who was most known for his biographical novels of artists such as Van Gogh, once said, "When I have trouble writing, I step outside my studio into the garden and pull weeds until my mind clears. I find weeding to be the best therapy there is for writer's block."

What Irving Stone was doing was walking away from the problem and allowing his unconscious brain to work it out while he did something completely different. This allows one's alpha waves to rise while doing a mindless chore, which in turn can crank up our creative moments.

To prove this theory, a research study looked at two different groups of people. Group one was put under stress. I'm not sure what kind of stress, but I'm glad I wasn't part of that study. Group two was allowed to relax. Then both groups were given a puzzle to solve.

What researchers saw was that the stressed group couldn't figure out the answer to the puzzle, while the other group, once their alpha waves began to rise, was able to answer the puzzle correctly.

What's happening is the alpha waves are allowing our brain to connect ideas that we hadn't thought of before. Why is all of this important for writing?

Because the more creative we are in writing our novels, the better and more engaging we can make our stories. So, the idea here is that if you feel stuck, don't just sit at your desk. Get up, move around, do something relaxing and non-taxing to your brain. However, don't go on social media or turn on the TV because those mediums feed your brain with information and don't let your alpha waves perform in a way that's necessary for creative thought. Instead, color in a coloring book, take a walk, or maybe, like Irving Stone, pull weeds in the garden.

What else can you do if you feel stuck? Go out and observe things as well as people. Ideas for characters, incidents, and locations might come to you from your observations.

For example, while at a coffee shop, I observed a woman wearing Disney princess headphones. Did she borrow her kid's headphones or her niece's? Or maybe she just loves princesses. A few weeks later, I observed a different woman at the laundromat sitting under the counter while there were plenty of chairs to sit in.

While these things by themselves are slightly quirky, I've considered combining those observations into the same character in a future story.

In another observation, I watched a young man at a

coffee shop licking his fingers every time he turned the page of a magazine. He was standing at the counter looking through magazines piled up for anyone to read. He was dressed in business attire--long-sleeved shirt with white and light blue pinstripes, his pants were dark, and he was wearing a belt. I had to wonder, was he seriously interested in the magazine or is he thinking of a way to talk to the pretty woman sitting in the chair next to him?

What does this mean for my writing? I could use this character in my story. In fact, I was looking for a character who draws attention to himself in a way that's nonchalant, and I think this is how he'll do it.

When you feel stuck, take a break. Do something relaxing, go people-watch, or make observations about the world around you--and you might just come up with a new idea.

For today's writing practice, use an observation of the world in your latest novel, and don't forget to take a break if you need it.

# The worst thing that can happen

You've spent a lot of days writing. That's amazing!

Today is a new day, so let's move on to a new idea. You should throw the worst thing that can happen at your main character. Why? Because it might just make the story better. And I'm not talking about killing the character, because that would probably end your novel. Instead, throw them into a different, worst possible situation.

For example, I saw this same writing prompt when I was writing *Toy of the Gods*. What happened? My character had been thinking about her old boyfriend and how she was glad he was out of her life. So in the next chapter, she finds out that he's on the trip into the Amazon, and she has no way to back out of the trip. To her, at that time, it was the worst thing that could happen to her.

By adding her ex-boyfriend, I created a greater depth to the story and took it to unexpected places. It also added a new plot that I hadn't considered before.

In another example, in Anne McCaffrey's *Crystal Singer*, her main character experiences the worst possible thing on the first page of the novel. She's been practicing to become a singer all her life, but her maestro informs her that she will never be a major player in the singing world, that it's time to move on. The problem is, she's never considered anything else and has no idea what moving on means. It plummets her into a self-identity crisis, and then the whole novel becomes a story of discovery and recovery to find a new life.

Where will the worst possible situation lead your character?

When faced with the worst possible situation, your character will have to deal with:

**A dilemma with something at stake:** In my example, Leslie realizes that her ex-boyfriend will be on the trip into the Amazon. What's at stake? Her autonomy and the respect she was not given because this was kept a secret from her.

**A choice:** Her choices are pretty limited. She can leave or stay.

**Choose an action:** Her first action is to try and to steal a Jeep from the remote location, but she can't get it to work, so she ends up not being able to follow through with her perfect choice. She's left with only one choice: Face her boyfriend, and find out why he's there.

**Face the consequences:** The consequences of her being stuck is she's forced to communicate with her ex and face off with the captain, who kept it all a secret, and face it with dignity. Well, mostly dignity.

If the whole situation is easy, then it's probably not a dilemma. Also, you want something that will either deepen and advance the plot of the novel, or it will reveal something about your character. Or, hopefully both.

In what way could a dilemma reveal character or advance the plot? It depends on the consequences. Your character could undergo a spiritual change, could recognize new possibilities in life, could gain a new appreciation of life, could build mental strength, or could experience a change in their relationships.

So, again: Give your main character a dilemma, a choice, an action, and consequences.

# Exploring New Characters

Hello, there! Welcome back.

Today, I want to talk about characters again. Specifically, do you have all the characters you need in your story?

For example, many great novels have three characters who are portrayed predominantly in the book. That includes *Harry Potter* with Harry, Hermione, and Ron, and *The Great Gatsby* with Jay Gatsby, Daisy Buchanan, and Tom Buchanan.

If you have three predominant characters, are you using them to their best possible attributes? What I mean is, are your characters working against each other in any way? Because if everyone is happy with each other and with all the same goals it's going to be B-O-R-I-N-G.

For today's writing practice, I'd like you to write a new scene where either a new character is added or maybe you dive into one of the three predominant characters you already have.

Whether you are adding a new character, or just building on a current one, here are some things to have them do:

- Introspection. What is your character thinking about
- Strong opinion. There's no interest or depth to a story if everyone is in agreement. Conjure up a disagreement between a character or characters.
- A secret. Nothing like having a secret that a character is keeping from others to make things interesting.
- Complexity. Is one of your three characters an antagonist? Show them in a good light; let us know that their character is complex and not just one-sided.
- Vulnerability. Are any of your characters vulnerable? Perhaps it's time to make them so.

That's a lot to think about for a character or set of characters. Go ahead and start a new chapter or page; set your timer for ten minutes. If you add a new character who you feel works for the story, make sure to create an outline about the character.

# Talking High Tech in Your Story

Do you have real or imagined tech in your story? For example, *Jurassic Park* is based on the idea of gene manipulation to develop dinosaurs. In this case, the tech isn't the main part of the story, but the premise wouldn't make sense without it. Otherwise, how would you make sense of dinosaurs roaming a Costa Rican island? Because of the tech, we see a well-funded entrepreneur, a mad scientist, and plenty of greedy characters out to get their hands on the tech. But the real story is the characters who are trapped on the island and attempt to escape.

The thing to note about *Jurassic Park* is that the writer never gets into the nitty-gritty of gene manipulation. He uses it as a plot device, and it adds another level of interest to the novel. The novel was also released during a time when gene manipulation was a big topic of discussion and concern.

*Ready Player One* is another example of tech used in a novel. It focuses on virtual reality. A timely and interesting topic. Do we ever hear about how everything works? Not really. The reader is given the general idea, and as individuals who have knowledge about virtual reality or have seen it on TV, we can fill in the blanks with our own ideas or we can withhold disbelief.

What I'm trying to say is that you don't have to get into the minute details of any tech in your story. As a sci-fi fan, I appreciate it and feel it's fun to incorporate tech into a storyline.

Don't have anything high-tech? Consider other things in your world that people might not understand right away and might need a little background information about.

Or maybe the highest tech you have is a cell phone or a sharp sword or maybe a smoke signal. That's still something you could incorporate into your story.

What about taking a moment to talk about that tech but in a way that folds into your story? In other words, you don't want to slam the reader with a lot of information, so be sure to write it so that it feels part of the natural flow of the story. How to do that? Have one or more characters interact with the tech.

For example, in Piers Anthony's *On a Pale Horse*, the main character, Zane, must quickly learn how to use his new ride, a flashy, specialized car that belongs to whoever holds the title of Death. He doesn't receive a user manual or instructions; instead, he's got to learn how to use it while on the job for the first time as Death.

It's your turn to connect your characters with tech--or at least get as tech as you can with your story.

# Using Prompts

Hello, everyone. Today, I want you to take a deep breath, and exhale, and smile. This writing process is amazing, and you're making it work. Do you feel like a writer yet? You should. You should take a look at those affirmations you wrote down in the first section of this book and repeat them out loud. You are a writer.

Now, writer, let's talk about writing prompts. Prompts are a way to give you new ideas for your story, but they should also give you enough freedom to fit the idea to your own story. They can also inspire new stories, help you develop your writing skills, and can create new directions you never even thought of.

I'll give you a few writing prompt suggestions. You can use one of these prompts in your story if you'd like--or jot them down to use later. Don't feel you have to use them exactly, but take one that goes well with your story-line and adds to your plot.

Here are those prompts:

- Someone has left an important note on a table for your main character. A window or door opens, and a gust of wind comes and lifts it into the air. What happens next?
- An animal has exposed something that one of your characters once hid and never wanted anyone to find.
- Your main character finds out something amazing about someone they've hated, and it changes their opinion of them. Or maybe they really liked the character, and the thing they found out changes their opinion of them in a bad way.
- Your main character has just been through something harrowing. Perhaps they almost died; perhaps they lost someone close to them. Then the main character gets yelled at by a boss or co-worker. What's their reaction?

And here are a few thought up by author, Elisabeth Loya:

- Your main character and their arch nemesis are forced to engage with each other at a social function where they must be civil. Describe the situation and how they get out of it.

- Your main character starts to doubt a core belief. What is it, what causes them to doubt, and how do they reaffirm or reject this belief?
- Your main character encounters their greatest fear. What is it, and how do they control their fear? Who helps them and how? This does not have to be a living/tangible person or thing; it could be a memory.

If you need more prompt ideas, you can Google and find a million to choose from, but I also believe that pulling in creative ideas you've come up with on your own will bring your novel to life in your special way. In other words, if you have any ideas waiting in your idea notebook, maybe pull one of those out and work on it.

# Read to Write

∞

Throughout this book, I've mentioned examples from other novels. Some of them because I loved reading them; some because they have great examples to share.

William Faulkner said, "Read, read, read. Read everything--trash, classics, good and bad, and see how they do it. Just like a carpenter who works as an apprentice and studies the master. Read! You'll absorb it. Then write. If it is good, you'll find out. If it's not, throw it out the window."

I like that part, and yes, throw bits of it out the window if they are terrible, which they might be. But don't do this until the editing phase.

But back to reading. I definitely suggest reading examples of the genre you're writing. But I think that also reading other genres can give us insight into good writing techniques.

By reading, we gain inspiration and ideas, as well as

insight into writing. Writing is also not something easily learned. It takes practice, hard work, and absorbing all those great examples that already exist. So many before us went through all the hard work, and now we just have to learn from them.

Not only that, research has shown, as Psychology Today notes, that "Neuroscientists have discovered that reading a novel can improve brain function on a variety of levels." So we're doing things that are good for our brain when we read.

And I hear it from writers and non-writers alike. They'd all love to read more. If that's you, I suggest challenging yourself to reading a certain number of books a year.

How to keep up with that challenge? Join a book club, or maybe start your own. By meeting with other people to discuss a book, it forces you to be ready and get that book read. Another option is to join a Goodreads reading challenge. Sign onto Goodreads, and look for the challenge option. Just make sure to give yourself a number that's obtainable. For me, reading 12 books in 2018 was a challenge but was doable. Then each time you finish with a book, note that on Goodreads, and keep reading.

But what about your writing challenge today? I have two for you. One, if you don't already have a book that you're reading, decide what book you'll start reading. And two, write for ten to twenty-five minutes, and make progress on that story.

# Writing a Prologue

Before I get into the writing of a prologue remember, this is your book, you can have a prologue if you want to. Just make sure you're using it to the best possible advantage for your story and your reader.

Often your main character does not appear in your prologue. Think of it this way, you have an opportunity in a prologue to build suspense for the reader. The reader is privy to information that the main character doesn't know.

Use a prologue to share something that's important to the plot that happens before the meat of your story.

You can foreshadow something as well as make sure that the tone of your prologue matches your genre – thriller, mystery, romance, etc.

My favorite prologue is in Julie Czerneda's Species Imperative book 1. It's two pages and it's powerful.

In Julie Czerneda's book, you see that something

somewhere is destroying planets – melting the plants and animals and drinking it up and it's hungry for more.

Then the story starts about a week later when a scientist is enlisted to help figure out what's killing planets. No one knows, they assume it's some type of weapon, but we the reader know that it's something more organic than that and that it's something that works quickly.

What you don't want to do is use a prologue to info dump. If you've written an initial chapter of your book that spends the whole time explaining why things are the way they are you probably need to delete that chapter or copy it into your research files because it's going to bore your reader.

Or take that chapter and intersperse the information throughout the story when the reader needs it.

I think that there's a lot of argument over whether you should have a prologue because some authors will use it as an info dump. And if you can't tell if it's an info dump, give it to your review group to tell you where the real story starts.

I know often I'll find that the real story doesn't start for a few paragraphs or a chapter beyond where I actually have it start.

And, don't feel bad if you have info dumped when writing a prologue. It's pretty normal. I find myself doing that less and less as I recognize when I'm info dumping.

So, I have two possible writing projects for you here.

1. Take twenty minutes and write the backstory to your story - what are the rules, how do things work. Then

put this as "research" but not a chapter in your book. Or find ways to intersperse this information throughout the book when the reader needs it.

2. Start your timer and write a prologue. What happened long ago or weeks before the main story begins that we need to know. Was it a spy passing along secret information (but the spy dies and so our hero enters the story searching for the information?); Was it an alien landing on earth but it gets picked up by another alien and leaves its spaceship behind? (Then our hero finds the derelict space ship, fixes it up, and becomes a space pirate?)

Get writing!

# Write the Beginning

Blaise Pascal said, "The last thing that we find in making a book is to know what we must put first."

Well, maybe it's not the absolute last thing we find in writing a book, but often it can be. Earlier, I talked about starting anywhere in your story, so you might not have written the first chapter yet (not counting the prologue.)

If you've already written your first chapter, when I give you your writing goal for today, I suggest you write it again, and then incorporate the two together when you edit, whether it's a month or two or more from now.

Here are some things you should consider when writing your first chapter:

- Make sure you set the scene for the whole novel in your first chapter. If your novel is an adventure thriller, then that first chapter had better hint at that. If instead, the first chapter feels like a romance, you're not going to keep your reader because they read the book jacket, and they want adventure thriller. If they see romance in the first few pages without a hint of an adventure thriller, they'll either think they picked up the wrong book or that your novel isn't living up to your book jacket. No one wants to feel that they've been taken for a ride, so make sure you're being authentic to your audience and your novel.

- Don't word-vomit in your first chapter (or any chapter, really). What I mean is, don't write several pages that explain your world, or the story, or the character. Instead, write the story in a way that shows us what's going on and how it works from the character's perspective. If you feel the need to write a multipage description about your world, use it for notes to help you remember things, but don't use it as your first chapter.

- This is from my friend and author Elisabeth Loya: Try to make your first chapter feel like a short story that reveals the slice of life that illustrates your characters' struggles and/or routines.

- I'd like to add to that: As a short story, it should be able to stand on its own, but the end should also want people to keep reading and find out what happens next.

. . .

Another thing to consider: Take a look at four or five favorite books, and peruse the first ten pages. Write notes down as to what you like about the beginning chapters. What works? What doesn't?

You might have already guessed your writing assignment for today. Write your first chapter, again, if needed. If you also want to write some back story to your world building, feel free to work on that too.

Keeping in mind, tell the story, and don't mind dump. If you still don't get the difference between back story and the story from the character's eyes, don't worry too much. Have your review group help you with that in the future.

# External Forces

External forces can include several options. Most of us would probably consider external forces to be nature and what she can throw at us. Physics would say that external forces include things such as gravity and friction. In literature it could be a struggle between the protagonist and another character.

It could be any of those things, where an external force is an obstacle to the protagonist reaching their goal.

The external forces in *The Lord of the Rings* include weather, like the snowstorm on the top of the mountain that forces our protagonist and his band to go a different direction, making it more difficult for them to reach their objective. The Orcs are also an external force.

In my own novel, *Toy of the Gods*, I throw a whole bunch of external forces at my protagonist, including rain, mudslides, and drunken monkeys.

There's so much that can happen to our characters in

our story. External forces are something that can definitely get in the way of our characters completing their goal.

I think you can tell that in the examples I used, the external forces came naturally from the genre as well as from the locations. What external forces would come naturally in your genre, location, and/or with your characters?

If you have a bunch of cowboys in the Wild West, you probably don't want your external force to be an alien abduction. Oh, wait, that's a bad example. Or maybe that's exactly what your story wants. If your story is absurd on purpose, you might want a giant space-flying squid, maybe a sea serpent, or maybe a giant duck has been set loose in the city.

Or, if you want something more down to earth, here are some other options to think of throwing at your characters:

- A natural disaster, as in *The Perfect Storm* by Sebastian Junger.
- A non-natural disaster like a water main break or an oil spill or zombies like in *World War Z* by Max Brooks.
- A direct conflict between the protagonist and the main antagonist. Think Harry Potter vs. Voldemort.
- An unjust law or government like in *The Hunger Games* by Suzanne Collins.

- A direct conflict between the protagonist and someone else who means well but ends up being an obstacle. Think Mr. Collins in *Pride and Prejudice* by Jane Austin.
- A direct conflict between the protagonist and minor antagonists. Think Frodo vs. Orcs or Harry Potter vs. Draco Malfoy

There you go. Today, of course, I want you to write about an external force. Good writing!

# Writing Thriller

There are techniques for creating thriller books that readers just can't put down. That page-turning story that they'll stay up all night to read.

Here are the tips to do just that: Page turning books are those that create suspense. You can do that by having a ticking clock (in other words something bad is going to happen unless the characters solves the problem fast)

Show the reader important things that the protagonist doesn't know (that can come from a point of view of your antagonist) - maybe we see them scheming their evil plans unbeknownst to our hero or heroine Make characters that readers care about and don't want bad things to happen to them — and bring in subplots.

I have a lot of characters in my books and that helps to create subplots because every character has their own goals and those goals don't mesh with each other which creates subplots.

When you're writing a scene that's particularly suspenseful or high energy like a chase scene – you should use shorter sentences. This means that the readers is moving faster through the story and they can feel the energy. You also don't want any internal thoughts or monologues or anything in that scene that's going to slow it down.

When it comes to page turning chapter endings, I've had people tell me that I do this really well. That when they get to an end of one of my chapters, they are more than likely to turn the page because they must know what happens next. I think I learned how to do this just from reading a lot from other authors who do this well.

Most of the time, I don't leave my readers with a cliffhanger at the end of a chapter, I think if you do this too much your readers would get a little exhausted. Instead, I leave them with a question, an unknown that they want to know more, or a what if, or it's a hint at what's to come. There is that occasional cliff hanger though.

International Award winning Southern Gothic Mystery writer and author of A Curse of Silver and Blood, writer Kimberly A. Banks. Had this to share about page turning thrillers.

"Be cruel; dangle your character over any metaphorical cliff you find. Create horrible situations that let your audience emotionally relate to them, and when your character loses their footing, end the chapter. It's human nature to search for answers to the unknown, and when readers are denied answers, they keep going until they find them. So, pose questions that will have answers later that rip your audience's feet from under them and cause them to fall head first into your story alongside your character."

And if Kimberly A Banks is anything like me, she's probably actually thrown a character off the cliff.

Today, start your timer and write one or more of the following:

1. A scene with your antagonist. We see them scheming some evil plan that puts our protagonist in jeopardy.

2. Write a scene where the protagonist learns that there's a time limit (maybe someone is injured and needs help or they'll die; maybe they are running out of food or water; maybe if they don't stop the bad guy the whole world will be destroyed!)

And at both endings, leave a hanging question over the head of the reader.

# Writing Romance

Romance can come in all sorts of scenarios; from casual flirting to outright sharing of affection.

If you're thinking of adding some romance to your story, go back to your character development. Which characters will work for this?

If you haven't been building up romance between the characters yet, put in your notes to go back and start building it between those characters. How? That depends.

Will these characters be going from enemies to lovers? Long time friends to devoted partners? Complete strangers to deeply in love?

Watch a movie or read a book where the characters progress into romance and take note. Did they start with casual flirting? If so, come up with ways your characters can flirt but still have the story plot move forward.

Using the backstory of the characters, you'll need to decide what that will look like.

Is your whole book focused on romance? Then don't forget the romance formula. Two people meet, fall in love, then something prevents them from getting together, but then against all odds they overcome it to be with each other. It should also end with a happy ending - no one wants to read romance to end up with an unhappy couple.

The crux of any romance is that the characters need to make each other feel deep feelings - anger or love. Anger? Definitely. That old enemies to lovers trope is exactly that. Who better to have a romance than two people who started out hating each other.

Here are some ideas to kick off the feelings toward romance:

Anger-

- One has badmouthed the other (Think Pride and Prejudice)
- One doesn't trust the other or has reason to think they're the enemy (even though they aren't)

Love-

- They've done something unbelievably difficult (like saving the other person's life)
- They've done something unbelievably sweet (like take them out on the best date ever)

Now, if it's just flirting you're after for your characters, your main character should first notice something about the other character that they like. Their eyes, legs, abs, something that we know there is some subtle physical attraction.

The main character needs to know that the other character is available (aka not in a relationship). And, that the other character is also interested, even if it's just a smile.

Casual flirting could be simple compliments they give each other, casual touches on the arm, that need to touch and connect.

Set your timer and write a chapter where you focus on the romance between the characters - whether it's just a little flirting, or things are getting deeper.

# Writing Sex Scenes

If you are not planning on writing a sex scene, go ahead and skip this chapter. But if that's something you'll want to do, this chapter is here to help.

Oh, boy, sex scenes. The first time you write a sex scene, it's like writing for the first time. It's also like having sex for the first time. Where do you put your hands, what's going to happen next, what happens with well, you get the idea. So don't be surprised if it's a little hard at first. Yes, pun intended.

My friend who writes paranormal romance as Trinity Tarrow told me that the first sex scene you write is always the most difficult. Also, after she read one of my sex scenes from a first draft of *Toy of the Gods*, she directed me to a list of words to use for body parts in sex scenes.

When I wrote my first one, it was awful, and it took a lot of input to make it better. So, I just want to give you some ideas to make it better from the beginning.

First, take a look at what you don't want to end up with. Google "Bad Sex in Fiction Award."

Second, what to do: Start off with a clinical look at what's happening. What movements will your characters make throughout the scene, and write that down as a list.

For example: "Donald gently grabs Lisa's arm. Lisa looks into Donald's eyes. Donald closes the door to the hallway. Donald holds Lisa against the wall. Lisa kisses Donald."

Now, turn that list into sentences that include feelings and details.

"Donald gently wrapped his hands around Lisa's arm. She looked up at him with longing in her eyes. Donald couldn't stop the flood of desire that poured into his heart from that look. He closed the door to the hallway behind him, leaving them to the private space. He pressed her to the wall, and she didn't hesitate to kiss him, running her fingers through his hair while pulling him closer."

Well, that's not perfect, but I think you get the idea. If your scenes go beyond kissing and foreplay, I'd say Google "terms to use in erotic fiction" because you don't want to use the same word over and over for the same body part - it gets a little tedious and no one wants a tedious sex scene.

And there you go. Figure out the steps first, and then wrap details, feelings, and magic around the scene so that it feels genuine.

Time for you to try your hand at a sex scene.

# Writing Fight and Chase Scenes

Chase scenes and fight scenes have a lot in common, they need to keep the reader wanting to know what happens next; they should be thrilling and nerve-racking; and there's that realism that pulls the reader in so they can feel what our character is going through.

Think about a time where your adrenaline was pumping. For me, I think about the time I was in Panama, and my friend and I had gone to the store and then wandered around the city. When we arrived back at our hostel, there was a closed gate about a hundred feet from the actual door. There was no way for us to get someone's attention, and we didn't have working cell phones. Luckily, the owner was walking out as we stood there trying to figure out what we were going to do.

Could you imagine that as part of a chase scene? Two young women in an unknown town walk in on something unexpected and then run for their lives being chased by henchmen, heading to their only safe haven, only to find that it's locked up tight, and there's no way to contact anyone. They have no choice but to keep running.

In addition to having standards, at the heart of every good chase scene or fight scene is simplicity. We don't want to hear a lot of internal thoughts from our characters or anyone waxing poetic over their weapon. There needs to be nonstop gritty action. Leave the deep thoughts and waxing poetic for after the scene when the protagonist is cleaning up their wounds.

Here's what I want you to do:

- Start a scene that evokes the feeling you're going for. If this is a spy novel, you can make your character feel that everyone is watching them. Which they are, because it's a spy novel.
- As soon as your characters clash or chase, it should be nonstop action. Unless your character is James Bond or Dr. Evil, wherein you'll add snide remarks throughout the scene.
- Use the location to its fullest. If there are lots of twists and turns, use them. If there's a lot of glass around, break it.
- Make sure danger is involved. Could your protagonist be at risk of being killed? Kidnapped? Left for dead?
- Share sensory data. The smell of the burning tires from tight turns, the feel of plants hitting

your character in the face as they run after or
away from someone, the feel of hurting and
the knowledge that there will be a big bruise
tomorrow from that hit to the shoulder.

Excited to write that scene? I hope so. Go get it.

# Keep Writing, and Don't Panic

There might come a time where you look at what you've written or you think about all the stuff you've written, and you suddenly panic and think it's all crap and that it's not worth writing. You're only half right. In truth, everyone's first draft is crap. But that first draft is words-on-the-paper kind of crap that you can take and edit later. Right now, it's just about getting all those words, the crappy ones and the amazing ones, all down together. Is it worth it? Yes. Whether you're working toward publication or you just want something for family, or just yourself, you've come a long way. So keep going.

Not finished writing the novel yet?

- Go back through this book and use the ideas to help you keep going.

- Take a look at your plots and subplots. What storylines are missing? Continue those storylines until you've completed them.
- If there are missing scenes in the middle of your story, write the scenes to connect everything you've written so you have one flowing story.
- Put your book through a critique group - other writers can often help you find what needs to be added (or subtracted from a story)

Meanwhile, I will share some words of encouragement.

"However great a man's natural talent may be, the art of writing cannot be learned all at once." That was said by Jean Jacques Rousseau, a philosopher and writer from the 1700s. So true, and we can learn from so many things, reading other people's work, joining a writing critique group with the right stuff, and the whole editing process. But you're also learning right now with every sentence you write for your story.

The next words of wisdom are from J.B. Priestley. "Most writers enjoy two periods of happiness--when a glorious idea comes to mind and, secondly, when a last page has been written and you haven't had time to know how much better it ought to be." Mostly, that's true. I'm hoping, that like me, you love it when you've written the last page of your novel in draft form but that you also know that editing will come in the future. And I bet you'll have plenty of ideas come to mind, and I hope plenty of times where you write that last page.

And if you're worried that no one will like what you're writing, here are some great quotes about that. Mickey Spillane, best known for his Mike Hammer novels said, "Those big-shot writers . . . could never dig the fact that there are more salted peanuts consumed than caviar." There was also a great meme on Facebook from @writers_write that said, "The next time you're worried your plot isn't good enough, remember somebody made money out of sharks in a tornado. . . ."

Octavia Butler once said, "No writer starts out great; the only way to become a great writer is through persistence."

And, one more.

"For several days after my first book was published, I carried it about in my pocket and took surreptitious peeps at it to make sure the ink had not faded"-- Sir James M. Barrie

I know what he means. Even after all the work, it was a surreal experience to see my book in print. I hope you'll keep writing and that someday you'll hold a copy of your book.

When the book is done, then start your editing process. Keep plugging away it and you'll get it done. Once your book is ready.

You can find my book on editing here: https://

sonjadewing.com/the-5-minute-author-how-to-edit-your-first-novel/

if you're considering self-publishing, check out my self-publishing workbook: https://sonjadewing.com/the-5-minute-author-self-publishing-workbook/

If you need support in writing or other writerly things, check out the Women's Thriller Writers Association. https://womensthrillerwriters.com/

Or check out my podcast, The Five Minute Author - on Apple podcast and other channels! https://www.buzzsprout.com/2026597/11069507


Keep writing!

# About the Author

Sonja Dewing is a multi-award winning author, creative writer, and self-publishing guru. She's also an award winning publisher and founder of the Women's Thriller Writers Association. She loves adventure, and living in Albuquerque, New Mexico.

You can find her fiction and other books on her website at www.sonjadewing.com

You can also find her business page here https://womensthrillerwriters.com/

www.ingramcontent.com/pod-product-compliance
Lightning Source LLC
Chambersburg PA
CBHW051029030426
42336CB00015B/2782